The Gospel According to Gipper

Joe Hamlet

Innovo Publishing

Published by
Innovo Publishing, LLC
www.innovopublishing.com
1-888-546-2111

Innovo Publishing

Providing Full-Service Publishing Services for
Christian Authors, Artists & Organizations: Hardbacks, Paperbacks,
eBooks, Audiobooks, Music & Videos

The Gospel According to Gipper
Copyright © 2011 by Joe Hamlet
All rights reserved.

No part of this publication may be reproduced, stored in a retrieval system,
or transmitted in any form or by any means electronic, mechanical,
photocopying, recording, or otherwise, without the prior
written permission of the author.

Unless noted otherwise, Scripture taken from the New American Standard Bible®, Copyright © 1960, 1962, 1963, 1968, 1971, 1972, 1973, 1975, 1977, 1995 by The Lockman Foundation. Used by permission. The Holy Bible, New International Version®, NIV® Copyright © 1973, 1978, 1984, 2011 by Biblica, Inc.™ Used by permission. All rights reserved worldwide. Amplified® Bible, Copyright © 1954, 1958, 1962, 1964, 1965, 1987 by The Lockman Foundation. Used by permission. (www.Lockman.org) The Message. Copyright © 1993, 1994, 1995, 1996, 2000, 2001, 2002. Used by permission of NavPress Publishing Group.

Library of Congress Control Number: 2011934184
ISBN 13: 978-1-936076-82-6
ISBN 10: 1-936076-82-9

Cover Design & Interior Layout: Innovo Publishing, LLC
Cover Photography: Randall Elkins

Printed in the United States of America
U.S. Printing History

First Edition: July 2011

Dedicated to my wife, Carol

My best friend and helpmeet who encouraged me to write this book. Without you, it would have been a dog's life for Gipper!

I thank God for the day I laid eyes on you and you later said, "I do!"

Love,
Joe

Cover photography by:

Randall Elkins
Randall Elkins Photography
1004 West 1st North Street
Morristown, TN 37814
(423) 307-8592

www.randallelkins.com

How to Use This Book

The Gospel According to Gipper can be for individual reading and for small groups.

What I want readers to experience is that the God of the universe does reveal Himself through His creation. This includes pets.

Hopefully you will be blessed by the stories of Gipper. More importantly, I want you to experience God and His insights. My hope is that you will be blessed as He chooses to reveal His truth from a pet.

So how are you to read the stories of Gipper?

For me, some books were written as if I were the only person in the world who was to read them. The author seemed to be writing directly to me. The thoughts and insights that came from reading were personal, for me alone.

Other books that I read were meant to be shared with others. I needed people who could identify with what I was thinking and feeling. I needed to bounce my ideas off others and hear their feedback. These books led me on a journey that others were taking.

For the reader who is on a solo journey, the questions at the end of each chapter will help you focus on certain areas of your life. They are meant to take you on trails that perhaps you would not have chosen. They are meant for you and you alone.

For those who are dog lovers and want to share their journey experiences, the discussion questions can be shared with others. You may want to hear what they think. You may need others to listen to you. This is your season to connect with other pet lovers.

My suggestion is that you read *The Gospel According to Gipper* for yourself. If after the last chapter you see that you need to talk out the questions, ask another pet lover to also read the book. Set up times to meet. Keep it simple. Keep it confidential. What you have in common is that you love your pets. As someone is sharing his or her story, ask yourself if that is a truth or an insight that is for you. Make notes afterwards.

So, what do I want for you after reading about a dog and his owner? I want you to have a greater awareness of God and His truth. Just as God brought Gipper into my life, maybe He has allowed you to be a pet owner in order to know Him better.

Each chapter has "gentle reminders." The idea of including gentle reminders comes from a flight I had taken over the Atlantic Ocean. My wife, Carol, and I were traveling to South Africa for our first mission trip. Before leaving, our son, Chris, handed me a letter. He told me to open it after we were in the air. His letter began with the phrase, "some gentle reminders." In his own handwriting, he listed Bible verses, one after another. Some of them were new for me; others were gentle reminders of what I already knew. While we traveled 30,000+ feet in the air on a dark night over the Atlantic, it was refreshing to have some *gentle reminders.*

And this is my prayer for you . . .

Father,
I'm not sure how You want to use the life stories of a dog in the lives of those who read this book. I do know that what You showed me was "good news" from the life of a dog. I was blessed. I want the same for others. Help them to see You in a new way through Your creation of pets. Use the Gipper stories to reveal Yourself to them. What You reveal to them, I pray will "make You look good." Blessings on those who love their pets! In the name of the One who created all the animals of the world, Amen!

—Joe Hamlet, 2011

Introduction

Why the title, *The Gospel According to Gipper*?
Why another book that has "The Gospel According to . . ."?

There's *The Gospel According to Peanuts*, *The Gospel According to ESPN*, *The Gospel According to Disney*, *The Gospel According to the Simpsons*, and lest we leave them out, there are the gospels according to Matthew, Mark, Luke, and John. If you want more book and article titles with "The Gospel According to . . .," Google that phrase and you will have more than a million matches.

So why another book about the "gospel?"

Because I needed some good news.

The meaning of "gospel" comes from the Old English word gōdspel, from gōd (good) + spel (tale). If you dig a little deeper, the "spell" in gōdspel, is from Middle English and means "to signify, ready by spelling letters."[*]

So what does this mean to this dog owner? It means that I needed some good news—some God-news. And it needed to be spelled out in the life of a dog named Gipper.

The Gospel According to Gipper is simply my passing this good news on to others. Some of it was new for me. Some of it was a "gentle reminder" of truths that I already

---

[*] Source is from www.merriam-webster.com/dictionary/spell

knew. A dog simply needed to remind me about what I already knew.

Blessings on you as you read. May what happened in my life with a golden retriever remind you that the God who created a dog named Gipper is the God who has good news for you.

—Joe Hamlet, Morristown, Tennessee, 2011

Table of Contents

How to Use This Book v

Introduction viii

1. How It All Began 13
2. Gipper and God's Commandments 17
3. Gipper in Dog Obedience School and Pet Owners in People Obedience School 23
4. Being a Dog 29
5. Taking the Longer Way 33
6. Petting a Dog . . . the Touch of God's Hand 37
7. Keep On Barking 41
8. When the Journey Is Long and Hot 45
9. Following the Right Path 51
10. God's Watchful Eye on You 55
11. Why Dogs Need Baths . . . and People Too 59
12. Waiting on God 65
13. Gipper and Fear 69
14. When Dogs Are "Bad Dogs" 75
15. God's Care as We Age 81
16. The Day Gipper Died 85
17. What Are You Leaving Behind? 93

Acknowledgments 99

1

How It All Began

It all started with a short prayer: "God, I would like to have a dog like that some day."

It was in the early 1990s. Our family was at the beach. One day, as we walked along the Atlantic, I saw a lady tossing something into the ocean. Her dog retrieved it. That's where it began: "God, I would like to have a dog like that."

That short prayer was soon forgotten. The children were young. I was a busy minister helping hurting families.

One Monday I passed the desk of a fellow employee, Sandra Valentine. She asked if I wanted a dog. I told her, "No. Too many things going on. I have no time for something else in my life."

Days later, Sandra said, "You know that dog I told you about? It is a golden retriever. The owner wants to give it away for free."

All of a sudden, there seemed to be room on that Monday for one more thing. I called John and Linda Hadden, the owners of the golden retriever. Linda answered the phone. She said they were moving to Texas, John was entering seminary, and their dog was not going with them. The reason? The Texas heat. They didn't think that a golden retriever with thick fur would survive the summer heat of Texas.

And why were they giving him away, no money involved? They wanted to choose the owner—an owner for their dog, of only a few months.

And his name? Gipper.

I asked if I could drop by their home. When I arrived, I met Linda and their son, Ben. Then I saw Gipper. He was in a fenced-in yard. I walked over to him and introduced myself. As I walked along the fence, Gipper followed me. It was love at first sight!

Some Fast Facts about Gipper:

- He was a beautiful golden retriever—registered.
- He wasn't just a dog. He was a DOG, 104 pounds of dog!
- Gipper was less than a year old. Lots of puppy still in him.

And if you know something about goldens, they are high-energy dogs. They like to dig holes in your yard. Many of them. They can't get enough of your attention. They bark at night. And when you take them out for a walk, you don't walk; you run. . . . and I did not know any of this about golden retrievers.

* * *

I thanked Linda for her time. When I got home, I told my wife, Carol, about Gipper. She was not that enthusiastic about the idea of a dog in our home, but soon warmed up to the idea.

Days later, the decision was made. We told the Haddens that we would like Gipper. They thought we would be good dog owners; we chose Gipper and they chose us to own Gipper.

I will never forget the day we picked him up. John had Gipper on a leash, approaching the house . . . one last walk. When I met John, I said, "I will treat Gipper like a million dollars." John's response? "He's worth more than a million." And that was prophetic. Little did I know that someday Gipper would be priceless.

The first night that Gipper was with us was like the first night of bringing a newborn baby home from the hospital. We tied him to a rope in the backyard and went to bed. In the middle of the night, we heard this awful dogfight. There was Gipper battling with one of the neighbor's dogs; it was a big dog that was part Chow.

I will never forget the sight. There was my wife running with a broom toward two fighting dogs, oblivious to the fact that all she was wearing was her nightgown!

We broke up the fight. There was Gipper. Our beautiful dog had held his ground. He was bloodied, but still wagging his tail. And what did I see? I saw a loving dog that could fight!

. . . and that's how it all began.

2
Gipper and God's Commandments

This book of the law shall not depart from your mouth, but you shall meditate on it day and night, so that you may be careful to do according to all that is written in it; for then you will make your way prosperous, and then you will have success (Joshua 1:8).

If I am asked, "What was your best decision about having Gipper as a pet?" I would say, "Choosing to have him." The second best decision? Buying an "invisible fence."

We knew that Gipper needed space. He was just one year old and had all the energy that one can imagine for a dog that was still a big pup. He needed to be contained in a place that gave him freedom to run, but we also needed to keep him under control.

We looked at different options: a kennel; a clothesline-type of device where Gipper, on a leash, could run in a straight line; chain-link fences; and the "invisible fence."

The decision was made—the invisible fence. The concept was inexpensive and practical. Running along our property line, a small, black wire was placed two inches beneath the soil. It was connected to a small box that sent out a signal to a "receiver" worn on a dog's collar. If a dog walked within a few feet of the property line, a chirp came from the receiver. It was a warning to the dog to move away. If the dog continued to move toward the black wire, a shock took place.

For about a month, we followed the training directions. Gipper was a smart dog, so he quickly caught on. No longer would we have to tie him up. He now had free run of almost one-third acre of property. He also knew that if he wandered near the road, he heard a chirp. If he did not move back into the yard, he received a shock.

Why did Carol and I spend money and time (the entire Labor Day weekend after getting Gipper) on a fence that no one could see? Some good reasons:

1. I knew Gipper would go crazy tied up all day. Not only that, but I knew that I would be mad at him for digging holes in the area where he was tied up (For the record, he never stopped digging holes and I did not stop getting mad).
2. Gipper needed a place to roam. As a high-energy dog, he needed an open front and back yard, which was plenty of space to move around.

3. It kept the neighbors from calling me, complaining about Gipper using their yard as a bathroom or getting into their trashcan. The invisible fence stopped that.
4. I did not want to worry about Gipper wandering away from home, wondering if and when he would return. And I sure did not want to spend hours driving around trying to find him.
5. And most importantly, I loved my dog. I knew Gipper would have a better life in our yard than what "out yonder" could provide. By staying close to home, we would always be there to provide for him. We knew he had it made in our yard.

So what does a dog and an invisible fence have to do with God's commandments?

What I wanted for Gipper, God wants for me. He knows a lot more about life than I do. He is very much aware of what life can do to me if I am left to wander on my own. He knows and He cares.

God knows He can provide for my daily needs. He has already bought the fifty-pound bag of dog food that will feed me for weeks. He knows what I like—dog treats sitting in a box that will last only a short time. He enjoys being with me and delights in "scratching my belly." And He will throw in a two-car garage for a doghouse. That is dog prosperity!

God knows the blessings for me . . . if I stay in the yard.

God gave us His commandments for two reasons: freedom and protection. Gipper was free to have a front and back yard. No confinement to a kennel or a five-foot leash. He was free to move around, but with limits.

God also wants to give us protection. Gipper had no "street savvy." He knew how to bark at a car, but he did not know that a car could run over him. I did. Gipper could wander off our property and have a great day sniffing out new sites. But I was not so sure that he could get back home like I could every day from work.

God's law and commandments are the same as an invisible fence. They offer us the freedom, but it is to the curb of life. He knows that if we obey Him and stay in the yard, we will have protection from the cars of life. He knows all of this, and more. He simply wants us to listen and obey. That is success.

Some Gentle Reminders . . .

- God knows we are limited in our knowledge about life. Because He knows our limitations, He often gives us limits for our limitations. It is for our protection.
- Pay attention to the "chirps" and "shocks" of life. We may not understand why our Owner trains us

to respond to chirps and shocks. We may not know why we can't go out into the streets. God does. Be submissive and content to His way of keeping you in your yard. Chirps and shocks are small prices compared to what could happen.

- Be thankful for all the things God has done for you, whether large or small. Be grateful for the bucket of water that is always filled, for the food He provides, and for the freedom to enjoy the space in the front and back yards. Be thankful.

- Take the time to know God's commandments. Study and know God's word. Meditate on it. Make the time to be still in His presence and ask, "Is there anything You want to reveal to me?" Know the One who has made you and all of life.

- And remember, all the boundaries, shocks, and limitations are there because God loves you. It is love that causes God to go to great lengths to provide and to protect. Know that He is loving when you see your limitations.

Discussion Questions

1. What have been some boundaries in your life that have limited you?
2. Have you been in training? What were the chirps and shocks that taught you about limitations in life?
3. Are there experiences for which you are thankful, thankful that God put boundaries in your life? How were you blessed afterwards?
4. Have you crossed boundaries and it cost you? Can you share this with someone so they will not pay the same price?

3

Gipper in Dog Obedience School and Pet Owners in People Obedience School

> *For they disciplined us for a short time as seemed best to them, but He disciplines us for our good, so that we may share His holiness. All discipline for the moment seems not to be joyful, but sorrowful; yet to those who have been trained by it, afterwards it yields the peaceful fruit of righteousness* (Hebrews 12:10–11).

A few weeks after Gipper came into the family, we realized that he needed training . . . a lot. We assumed that a few times of saying "No, don't do that!" would turn him into an obedient dog. Were we wrong!

We heard the announcement that our local community college was sponsoring a dog obedience school. We thought this was a great way to jump-start Gipper adjusting to family expectations.

Our first class was utter chaos, *utter chaos*. Gipper had never been around so many dogs in his life. Not only had he not seen this many dogs, but also he had never sniffed that many dogs! There was a continual tug-of-war between us; we were constantly pulling him away from his classmates. The tug-of-war was so bad that Gipper would cough because of tugging on his leash. As the class ended, I thought Gipper was "one of the dogs"—one that needed some training. I could not have been further from the truth.

When we returned for the second lesson, the two class instructors met with me before the class began. In the hand of one of them was a collar that I had never seen. Not only did it go around a dog's neck, but it went around his nose. When the dog tugged at the leash, his head went down, taking away some of the pull that a 104-pound dog would exert. This was the collar they recommended for Gipper.

I thanked them for their individualized attention and said that I would stop by their veterinarian clinic to pay for this special collar.

I put the new collar on Gipper and we joined the class. As I looked around at his canine classmates, I noticed that there was not one other dog with the same kind of collar. I was embarrassed. I had the problem child of the classroom!

Did the collar help? Oh yes. Did we have better control over our dog? Yes. We were most thankful that someone had invented such a device. But Gipper was the only dog wearing it. It seemed that the eyes of other dog owners were on him, the uncontrollable child, and me, the dog owner who needed a muzzle-like device to keep my dog from biting their dog! That one class made me realize how badly Gipper needed to learn obedience without my always having to pull on his leash.

We made it through dog obedience school. There were some mixed feelings at the end. I was thankful that Gipper learned some basic skills and thankful that Gipper was not sitting by dogs more obedient than he. On the last day, I bragged that our dog was the most improved student of the class.

As the years passed, we continued to use this special collar. Gipper did not resist. In fact, when he saw us with the blue leash with the special purple collar, he became excited. He knew he was heading out for a walk or run, and he was with those he liked. Whether it was a walk in the park or our sprinting behind him, we did not leave home without it. We were thankful for the collar that no other dog had used in obedience school.

But Gipper was not the only one who needed discipline. Years later, I learned that it is humans, the owners of dogs, who need the real training. It is the owners of dogs who need people obedience schools.

For you see, Gipper was simply responding to what I did or did not do. If I had not decided to attend dog obedience school, I would not have learned the basic commands to teach Gipper. If I had refused to follow through with training, Gipper would not have learned submission to a higher authority—me, the alpha dog.

There are three reasons why Gipper needed discipline. One, it was for his good. Obeying kept him out of trouble. He and I had similar expectations for appropriate behavior. I knew what was best. Two, it was for the good of others. There's nothing like an uncontrollable dog around people. Three, it was good for me. There is a oneness—a relaxed relationship between a dog and his owner when there is submission. We both enjoyed each other's company.

What both Gipper and I learned from each other is what God wants to teach us. The reason behind His discipline is that He honestly loves us. It is His love that motivates Him to spend time to discipline us.

The results of the personal discipline were twofold. The discipline was for our good. The discipline that Gipper received did not benefit any other dog. It was for his good.

The second result for discipline was that Gipper's behavior conformed to our expectations. His disciplined behavior was for both him and me. The same is true for us. God disciplines us so that we can "share His holiness"—we can be more like Him. Holiness is simply a separation from that which is not good for us—sin. God knows that when we are holy, we are separated from sin and close to Him. The world sees that we are different. We reflect who He is, one who is holy.

Did Gipper like discipline? I don't think so. And neither do I. I don't like it when I have to do things that I don't like, paying a price for changes in my lifestyle. At the moment, it really isn't joyful.

What makes it worth the cost are the results. When Gipper obeyed, there was a peaceful oneness. Things were just "so right" between the two of us.

That is what the Scripture says: the result of our godly discipline is "the peaceful fruit of righteousness" (**Hebrews 12: 10–11**). What happens to us is peaceful and righteous.

Some Gentle Reminders . . .

- When God disciplines us, it is because He loves us; there is no other motive.
- Most discipline, at that moment, is not enjoyable. Stay honest with yourself.
- Keep the end in mind. We develop endurance (**Hebrews 12:7**). We have a peaceful fruit that is righteousness (**Hebrews 12:11**).
- And the bottom line? We become more like God . . . holy (**Hebrews 12:10**). We separate ourselves from that which is not good for us because we love Him. There is a oneness within ourselves and

with Him that gives peace. We are simply one with Him.

Discussion Questions

1. Share some times from your past when you were disciplined. What did you do? What was the discipline? What were the results? Share the feelings that were felt during the process and afterward.
2. Have there ever been times that you were unjustly disciplined? What kind of pain did you experience? What scars were left?
3. Did you ever have discipline that produced favorable outcomes, peaceful fruits of righteousness?
4. Share some times that you disciplined your pet or a child. How did you know that you were doing the right thing? Did you ever have a time when you took discipline too far? Do you think God ever does that?

4

Being a Dog

Judas then, having received the Roman cohort and officers from the chief priests and the Pharisees came there with lanterns and torches and weapons. So Jesus, knowing all the things that were coming upon Him, went forth and said to them, "Whom do you seek?" They answered Him, "Jesus the Nazarene." He said to them, "I am He." And Judas also, who was betraying Him, was standing with them. So when He said to them, "I am He," they drew back and fell to the ground (John 18:3–6).

On more than one occasion, I would take Gipper out for a run around our circular neighborhood. It was more than a time to run. It was a time to sniff.

Goldens are blessed with an unbelievable "sniffer." On one particular trip, Gipper occupied himself with any of the hundreds of scents around him. Whatever caught his attention, he stopped to sniff.

During this stop-and-go run, dogs that were fenced in the neighbors' backyards spotted Gipper. They went crazy barking at him. As I jogged with a sniffing dog, we left a trail of barking dogs.

And what was going on with Gipper? He was oblivious to all the commotion. He was so unaware of his barking neighbors. Gipper was simply *being* a dog.

What does this have to do with Jesus as He faced a mob in the middle of the night?

When Jesus asked, "Whom do you seek?" They said, "Jesus the Nazarene." When He responded with "I am He," the literal translation in the Greek is "I am."

And what was the reaction of the mob when Jesus answered their question? They fell to the ground because of Who He was—the "I am." He could have called on 72,000 angels: "Or do you think that I cannot appeal to My Father, and He will at once put at My disposal more than twelve legions[*] of angels?" (**Matthew 26:53**).

Jesus could have told Peter to use his sword. He didn't *do* that either. Jesus simply acknowledges who He is—I am.

In Christian circles, we often think that our only influence on others is doing. If we don't "do something," we think we have not done God's will.

Does God command us to "do"? Yes. Jesus clearly states we are to "work the works of Him who sent Me" (**John 9:4**). We are to be obedient and do the work

---

[*]A Roman legion was composed of 6,000 soldiers. So this would represent more than 72,000 angels. In 2 Kings 19:35, a single angel killed more than 185,000 men in a single night. Source: *The John MacArthur Bible*, p. 1414.

of Christ. Yet sometimes, God wants us to be who we are—people who allow Christ to *be* in us. He simply wants others to see Christ in us.

And who are we? People who allow Christ, through the Holy Spirit, to be who He is—our life (**Colossians 3:4**).

The day we took our jog in the neighborhood, Gipper was being a dog. He wasn't doing anything to influence the other dogs. He was being who he was, a dog.

Some Gentle Reminders . . .

- If you are a Christian, you have Christ in your life. Let others see Him in you.
- To better understand who you are, take the time to better understand who Jesus is. We are made to be in His image and called to be more like Him.
- When you see trouble—a "mob"—coming toward you, ask, "Father, is there something You want me to do . . . or simply be who I am?"

Discussion Questions

1. How does a person discern between being and doing? How does one study Jesus, in order to be more like Him?
2. What kinds of "mobs" have come your way? What has been your reaction? Like Peter, did you cut off any "ears?"
3. In Revelation 19:14, we read that Jesus is coming back with the "armies of heaven." How does a person decide when to use an army of angels or simply be who he or she is?

5

Taking the Longer Way

Now when Pharaoh had let the people go, God did not lead them by the way of the land of the Philistines, even though it was near; for God said, "The people might change their minds when they see war, and return to Egypt." Hence God led the people around by the way of the wilderness to the Red Sea; and the sons of Israel went up in martial array from the land of Egypt (Exodus 13:17–18).

Gipper was a high-energy dog—a trait of goldens. That energy went somewhere . . . like digging holes in our front yard or his taking off at breakneck speeds when on a leash.

To get rid of some of that energy, Gipper was trained to run the long way around the house. I would show him a slice of bread, whistle at him, make a circle with my hand, and say, "Go." That was his cue to take off and run the long way around the house.

I then went the other way, a shorter way, about twenty to thirty feet. We met at the "petting area," a brick wall where Gipper would sit at eye level. There, I rewarded him with bread. Again, I whistled, made a circle with my hand, gave the command to go, and he took off, the long way around the house. I walked back to our first meeting place, the short way, and met him. He was rewarded with more bread. We did this until we ran out of bread.

Why all the running? Why did I make him run the long way? And what does this have to do with several hundred thousands of people traveling from Egypt to the Promised Land?

Gipper had no concept of the "big picture of life"; he had no idea what his digging or racing on a leash did to others. I did.

And it is that way with God. He has a bigger picture of your life than you do. He knows when the "longer way around" is best for you . . . and for others.

God knew His people well. He knew they were not prepared for the difficulties of war. He knew they would go back to the bondage of Egypt, the very place for which they had cried out for deliverance. And He knew there were future battles for them to win, battles that would give them a land of milk and honey. It was His will to prepare them.

And God knows you well too. He has plans for peace and hope for you (**Jeremiah 29:11**). When you are in a season of life when it is costing you twice as much and is taking twice as long, don't forget these "gentle reminders":

Some Gentle Reminders . . .

- God knows the bigger picture.
- He has plans for you, good plans for you, and they are better than your own.
- And God's plans are for winning the battles of life. Line up in "marital array" and walk with Him! (**Exodus 13:18**).

Discussion Questions

1. Are you stuck in some kind of Egypt? What would you like to happen for you to be free?
2. If you were freed from your Egypt, what would cause you to go back?
3. Is something taking you twice as long and costing you twice as much? How much has it cost you and how long have you been "traveling?"
4. What help would you like from others as you are "going the long way around?" And, what kind of help would you like from God?

6

Petting a Dog...
the Touch of God's Hand

Then some children were brought to Him so that He might lay His hands on them and pray; and the disciples rebuked them. But Jesus said, "Let the children alone, and do not hinder them from coming to Me; for the kingdom of heaven belongs to such as these." And after <u>laying His hands on them,</u> He departed from there (Matthew 19:13–15).

Gipper liked to be touched. One of my favorite memories is of Carol and me sitting on our deck. Gipper would park himself beside our chairs. If we did not pet him, he poked his nose under a hand or arm. This continued until the petting began.

If our hand became tired, he went to the other side of our chair. Same routine. If we did not pet him with the rested hand, he would put his nose under our hand or arm until we stroked him. And if "petting fatigue" set in, he went to the other owner!

It did not stop there. At times, Gipper would want more than a hand on his head. He would take his body and lean on us. He wanted more than a hand; he wanted bodies touching bodies, and so he would lean his body against us.

And sometimes all of this was still not enough. Our dog would roll over and want us to scratch his belly.

The touch of a dog owner—that is what Gipper wanted.

What about our wanting the hand of God on us? When are the times that we want His touch?

I don't think any of us are any different than Gipper. For all of us, there are the times when we need a touch and only the touch of God will do. Jesus knew this. That is why He rebuked His disciples and allowed the children to come to Him.

There was one other thing about Gipper wanting his pet time. When he came to us, he came with confidence. He did not have any guilt ("Oh, my master has petted me three times today. I feel so bad wanting him to pet me again."). No guilt. No shyness. He came with confidence.

And that is what God wants us to do. He wants us to come to Him for a touch. He does not mind our "noses" under His hand telling Him that we need His touch.

And our coming to Him is not always a necessity. It can be for a delightful touch. Whether it is a scratch behind the ear, or an I-will-always-love-it scratch on our bellies, God delights in extending His hand.

Some Gentle Reminders . . .

- To be scratched or not to be scratched, that is the question. Know yourself. Do you want a stroke on the head, a scratch on the belly? Know what you want and need. Maybe you need to lean in on the Master. Maybe there are days when you need "the works." Know thyself.
- Come to God with full confidence. The truth? God wants us to boldly come to His throne of grace in time of need to receive both mercy and grace (**Hebrews 4:16**).
- And remember, God's hand does not get tired!

Discussion Questions

1. What does it mean to for you to have the hand of God on you? What do you need from the hand of God in order to know or feel His love?
2. What causes a person to feel guilty for asking too much from God?
3. Think of a time when you have sought the hand of God when He wanted you to seek Him. What

is the difference between the hand of God and God giving Himself?

4. Have you heard the expression in the classroom: "That student is just acting out to get attention?" How do you put your "nose" under a hand to get attention? Have you used negative behavior in an effort to get attention? What happened? And if the results were negative, what are appropriate ways to do the right thing for future attention?

5. And if you see that you are still "negatively acting out," what lies underneath?

7

Keep On Barking

Keep on asking and it will be given you; keep on seeking and you will find; keep on knocking [reverently] and [the door] will be opened to you. For everyone who keeps on asking receives; and he who keeps on seeking finds; and to him who keeps on knocking, [the door] will be opened (Matthew 7:7–8, Amplified).

For some reason, Gipper never could sleep in a doghouse. No amount of treats tossed into a doghouse would woo him into it.

A "guy" dog owner would have simply allowed natural consequences with the weather to influence a dog's decision to use his newly bought doghouse. Enough rain and cold weather would convince him that his igloo-shaped house was the best place for him to sleep.

But noooooo, there are women who also are dog owners. My wife thought our garage would better meet Gipper's needs. By leaving the garage door up about two feet, Gipper could come and go in his much bigger doghouse.

Moving from a three-foot-diameter doghouse to a two-car garage doghouse presented a host of new problems. I'll never forget the night that we were awakened by Gipper having a good ol' southern conniption fit. A skunk had waddled into our garage. Gipper had him corralled behind the washing machine. He was doing everything that a dog could do to get the skunk.

As man of the house, I led my wife to the garage. It was 3 vs. 1—one couple in their pjs with a howling dog versus a skunk wondering whether to spray or not to spray. Carol was holding a dog going crazy. I was holding a broom, eyeballing a skunk. I then heard these famous last words from my wife: "I'll hold Gipper while you get the skunk!"

When Gipper was not dealing with a skunk, he was getting room service. He learned early that if he stood at the bottom of the steps leading to the garage, he could bark and get breakfast. Carol and I learned early that if we did not want a barking dog, we would stop what we were doing and feed him.

And you know what? Sooner or later, he got fed.

Some Gentle Reminders . . .

- When praying for God's will, keep on asking, knocking, and seeking. God has no problem with His children's need to be fed. Would Gipper "take a break" after continuous barking? Yes. Sometimes there are other things in life more important than feeding a dog (like sleeping in late!). But he kept barking. He barked until he was fed. God knows you have needs and godly desires. When I chose to have a dog, I took on the responsibility to care for him. God does the same for us. He will respond to you.

- What does it take for me to keep "barking"? I need to be reminded that God does love me. When I know that the God of the universe greatly loves me and knows what is best for me, I have hope. I have hope that He will bring my food bowl. With love and hope, I then trust Him. Faith, love, and hope. That is what I need to keep on asking, seeking, and knocking for my daily meal.

- When you are not immediately fed, don't be mad and/or sad. Not once did I see Gipper's anger because I was late. When his meal was brought to him, there was no sulking, or "I could bite your hand because I barked so long!" There was no you-don't-love-me look in his face. He didn't look at me as if to say, "Don't you touch me!" His focus was on the food bowl. The tail wagged because he saw the food.

- When I am hungry, frustrated, or tired, it's very tempting for anger and depression to overwhelm me. It happens. What I need are gentle reminders that God has fed me in the past. I need to be reminded that His character is good and loving. God wants us to recall what He has done. It gives us hope (**Lamentations 3:21**). And don't forget, He chose you; therefore, He is responsible for your care.

Discussion Questions

1. Were there times that you kept asking, knocking, and seeking, and God did not bring the food bowl? What kept you "barking?"
2. How do you deal with your anger when prayers are not answered? How did God respond to your anger?
3. What happens when sadness continues in your life? How do you keep spiritually barking?
4. How do you handle the God-does-not-love-me feelings? What did it take for you to fall in love with Him again, especially if you were weary of barking?
5. And if you are angry with God for His nonresponse, what would you want from others?

8

When the Journey Is Long and Hot

"Blessed is the man who trusts in the Lord And whose trust is the Lord. For he will be like a tree planted by the water, that extends its roots by a stream; and will not fear when the heat comes; but its leaves will be green, and it will not be anxious in a year of drought nor cease to yield fruit" (Jeremiah 17:7–8).

The local state park near our home is Panther Creek State Park, named after Panther Creek Springs that runs through the middle of the park.

One of the trails on which we would walk and jog is a two- to three-mile loop. It runs along the small stream fed by the springs. About midway was our take-a-break stop. The place was chosen because of a gentle slope leading to the stream.

Sometimes we would give Gipper a gentle tug in the direction of the stream. It was a gentle reminder to let him know that we were near his "drinking hole." On hot, summer days, no reminder was needed. Gipper knew where his "seventh-inning stretch" was, and he tugged us in that direction.

If you remember, Gipper's thick, golden fur was one of the reasons we got him. The previous owners were moving to Texas and they didn't think he could tolerate the heat. Thus, we became his new owners.

With his tongue hanging to one side of his mouth, Gipper went straight to the cool water. But he did not stop with simply lapping the water. Gipper took his thick coat of hair and plopped into the water. With water streaming around him, he would lower his head for repeated drinks.

When Gipper was done, we continued our jog to our car. It took us about one experience to learn that a stinky, wet dog does not go with the back seat of a car. Thus, a beach blanket became one of the accessories of our time together. As we drove home, we would turn our heads and check on him. Nothing like riding home in a stinky car because of a stinky, tuckered out, cooled-off dog!

God knows our journey in life is long and hot. He knows that we have fur that makes us most uncomfortable during the summer months. He made us that way.

God also knows that at times there are droughts. They can stretch from the summer into the other seasons. They last much longer than we would ever wish. And to make it through those seasons, He knows that we need water.

Because He knows all of this, He leads us to the cool water. It is His responsibility and He wants to do this for us.

So what can we learn from a dog?

Some Gentle Reminders . . .

- God allows the long trails of life and the "thick fur" that we wear. He understands that we get thirsty and need water. He wants to provide all we need to quench our thirst and for cool waters to revive us.
- It takes trust for us to have a safe, intentional, ongoing relationship with the Lord. For us to come into His way of providing, we need to let go of how we think we need water and come alongside of Him. He knows where the stream is and wants to lead us to it (**Psalm 23:2**).
- God knows that sometimes we need more than a drink. He knows that we need to "plop" into a stream to cool off. His provision is not just for us to drink from a trickle of water. He sometimes gives us more water than we could ever drink (**Psalm 36:8**). And when He does this, He delights in our cooling off from the drought.
- God provides continuously in life, one stream after another. He reminded Jeremiah that we are not to

- fear "when the heat comes and to be anxious in a year of drought." He will provide the streams.
- God sees the big picture. He sees that there is more to life than just drinking. He wants us to "be green" and wants us to produce fruit. That fruit is usually for both others and ourselves.
- And sometimes, God does more than provide the streams of life. Sometimes He provides bottled water. Carol and I often shared with Gipper our bottled water before reaching the stream. And yes, we did make sure that we drank first!

Discussion Questions

1. What kind of "thick fur" do you have in life that makes you miserable? What do you do to cool off? If you are still miserable, how can others help?
2. Do you remember times in your life when you were hot and thirsty? Were there experiences when God provided more for you than you expected? Share them with others or take time to write them down as future reminders. They can be "gentle reminders" when there are future droughts in life.
3. Are you on a long and hot journey? What is it costing you? How would you like God and others to reach out to you?

4. Have you, as a pet owner, known the satisfaction of watching your pet drink water that you provided? What did it mean to you and your pet?
5. Jesus said that if parents who are evil can give good gifts to children, how much more does our Father in heaven want to give us Himself, the Holy Spirit? (**Luke 11:13**). What do you think He meant? Have you experienced someone giving of himself or herself to you, not including a present? What does it mean to give not just a gift, but yourself?

9

Following the Right Path

He restores my soul; He guides me in the paths of righteousness for His name's sake (Psalm 23:3).

One of the reasons why Carol and I chose our house is its close proximity to Panther Creek State Park. It is a five-minute drive to the park. There are lots of trails for hiking and jogging. When Gipper came into our lives, he was part of this time in the park.

If there is a heaven to a dog, the state park was that for Gipper. As we approached the park, Gipper literally quivered with excitement as he saw the familiar surroundings. After parking the car, it took two of us to stop him from bolting out of the car. One of us would hold him in the car by the leash as the other slowly opened the door.

We learned that walking was not part of the agenda. Jogging was the pace. Why? Because Gipper pulled so hard on the leash as we walked. What a pace car is to the Indy 500, Gipper was to us. The difference is a pace car slows down the drivers. Gipper caused us to speed up. He was our pace dog!

What the neighborhood did not offer with scent, the trails made up for it. It was paradise for the olfactory senses of a golden retriever. If he was not running, he was sniffing.

By the end of the jog, Gipper was one contented dog. He was usually wet from lying in the creek that ran through the park. And was he tired!—his pink tongue hanging to the side of his mouth.

During the entire outing, Carol and I made the decisions. We chose when to go to the park and we chose which trails to take. Gipper had no part of the decision-making process. We knew the right trails to take. He did not.

What was Gipper's role? To obey. Although he was usually out in front, he knew to follow when the signal was given.

God is very much like that. There are a lot of trails in life. He knows which ones we are to take. He understands which paths of life are righteous for us. He is the Shepherd who guides.

Whether we identify with sheep in the **23rd Psalm** or with a golden retriever, we too need guidance. As much as we love our "state parks," there are so many things that can go wrong—too many wrong trails. We need the One who created sheep and dogs to lead us on trails that are right for Him and us.

Who has more fun on the trails, a dog or his owner? Hard to tell. I think that is true of God. He delights in us (**Psalm 22:8**). The One who made both dog and dog owner is the One who delights in you.

Some Gentle Reminders . . .

- It's God's desire to lead us on paths that are righteous. Let Him do this. He has a good reason . . . for the sake of His name.
- For Gipper to be part of the event, we had to keep him on a leash. Don't let the leashes of life fool you. There is a lot more freedom being on a leash in the hands of a dog owner who loves his pet than stuck behind a fence with no leash. God knows when we need limitations. He knows that we might not make it home if there is no leash. We need the guidance of our Owner.
- And it's nice to know that at times He gives us the freedom to run with all our might down the trails of life. God has no problem keeping up with us.
- And remember, sometimes God wants to give us more than a big yard. He wants to give us a state park!

Discussion Questions

1. Are you on any kind of a short leash? Limited income? Stuck in a job you hate? Are there any benefits for these limitations that might have blessings in disguise, blessings that offer more freedom?
2. If you could dream for the next five minutes, what is your state park, your heaven on earth? What would make you quiver with excitement? Can you share this with a friend who would pray about a park for your life?
3. Are there times in your life that you saw God guiding you down a righteous path? Share that with someone who will celebrate with you.

10

God's Watchful Eye on You

I will instruct you and teach you in the way which you should go; I will counsel you with My eye upon you (Psalm 32:8).

Looking at your dog. Your dog looking at you. Two sets of eyes meet. For a moment, nothing else exists. Those who love their dogs will understand what I mean. It is not scheduled on your calendar. It's not intentional. It just happens . . . your eyes are on the pet that you love. [Remember this moment. It will come up in a later chapter.]

One day I was in our driveway. Gipper was lying down at one of his favorite places—underneath the maple tree in our backyard. This was his spot on hot days. Gipper turned his head and my eye caught his. We made eye contact. It was brief. I smiled and he turned his head back around, returning to his world in the backyard. The words of the psalmist came to my mind: "I will counsel you with My eye upon you," says God.

If you have been in the presence of a godly counselor, you know what happens when the counselor's eyes meet your eyes. The eye contact takes place, the into-me-you-see encounter is experienced, and the needed wisdom, knowledge, or understanding is given. The focus is on the eyes, nowhere else.

If I, a finite dog owner, can enjoy a moment of my eye connecting with my dog's eye, how much more does the One who made both dog and dog owner enjoy looking at us? And how much more will we benefit from the personal encounter of One, the wonderful Counselor, who greatly loves us, who offers us the best of counsel?

Some Gentle Reminders . . .

- All pet owners are limited. We don't have all the time in the world to look at our pets. There is more to do in life than staring at our pets. God is not limited. He has the time and capability to keep His eye on us all the time. Nothing you do can escape His attention toward you. He is there.
- God does not simply want to look at you. He wants to instruct you, teach you, and counsel you. He goes to great lengths to reveal Himself to us . . . from bringing pets in our lives to sending His Son who best reveals Who He is.
- There are few things in life more frustrating than talking to a preoccupied person who is not listening. As you talk, his eyes are elsewhere . . .

and so is he. God is not like that. When He counsels you, offering what is perfect, He has His eye on you. You are the significant one for the moment.

- And what if Gipper's eye had not met mine? Chances are that you would not be reading this story. God keeps His eye on us. We are to keep our eyes on Him. How? We choose to come into His presence and focus on Him. We minimize the distractions and focus on the Creator who loves. When there is great love between two people, the eyes meet.

- The story is told in Jewish history about the city of Jerusalem surrounded by the enemy. The fearful king gathered the people to seek God's help. He said to God, ". . . For we are powerless before this great multitude who are coming against us; nor do we know what to do, but our eyes are on You" (**2 Chronicles 20:12**). God spoke through a prophet. The king and the people listened and obeyed. The next day when God's people arrived at the camp of the enemy, the entire army was already destroyed. It took them three days to bring the spoils of the enemy back to Jerusalem. The people kept their focus on God. Keep your eyes on Him.

Discussion Questions

1. When someone has his eyes on you, what are you thinking and feeling?
2. Research shows that the first thing that people do when meeting each other is to focus on their eyes. Is this also true of people with animals? Why do you think eye contact is important?
3. How does one sense God's eyes are on him? Do you have a story that you can share about when you focused on God and He on you?

11
Why Dogs Need Baths ... and People Too

Wash me thoroughly from my iniquity and cleanse me from my sin (Psalm 51:2).

If you have never smelled a dog that has not had a bath in months, then your olfactory senses have missed out on life. And if your dog that has not had a bath in months gets wet, you will have a memory that all other dog lovers fully understand.

I'm sure shorthaired dogs can stink after a certain period of time, but I think longhaired dogs have it over them. A dog owner knows when a bath is needed. You can have 1,000 things on your mind when your pet comes to you for a pat on the head. One whiff and you know it is bath time. Until that pet of yours is clean, no one is happy.

For Gipper, a bath was the highlight of his week. We dreaded that we would end up as wet as he, but he loved it. What happens in the movies happened to us. At some point during the bath, Gipper had to shake. At first, we were not prepared. We were not dressed for the occasion, with clothes that we knew could get wet and end up smelling like a dog bath.

He would sit on his back legs and let us do all the work. It was like a spa treatment—water flowing over him, someone washing every inch of fur. Like some teenage girl taking a shower, he would sit there under the water until we told him to "get out of the shower!"

Like a lot of other things we did for him, Gipper had it made. Not only did he have a scented shampoo bath, he got a conditioner added to his spa treatment. Not only did he have it "made in the shade" on a hot day, he had it made when the weather was cool. He had hot water.

As other dog lovers know so well, dogs don't sit there and appreciate all the hard work that goes into their bath . . . At some point in time, Gipper would get up, shake, and then roll in the grass. As we looked at green grass on his wet, clean fur, we realized that half of our efforts had gone to waste.

And this routine happened repeatedly. Yet year after year, Gipper got baths. Why? Two reasons:

1. We didn't like stinky dogs. Having a dog in our lives whose stink distracted us and others simply did not work.
2. Dogs get dirty. As a way of life, dirt got on Gipper; therefore, baths became a way of life.

"Getting a good cleaning" was good for both him and for us.

We humans know the same is true for us. We don't like feeling dirty and the smell that comes from our bodies. Those around us don't like it either. That is why baths are universal. People want them and need them.

That is also true for us spiritually. In **Psalm 51**, we read the confession of a man who committed adultery with another man's wife. To cover the affair, he had her husband killed. That is sin. And that stinks.

And who made this confession? King David, a man after God's own heart. David was now an adulterer and murderer. He had sinned. He knew he was unclean. After acknowledging and confessing his sin, he wanted to be clean.

But David did not settle for a sponge bath. He wanted to be washed "thoroughly." In **Psalm 51:7**, he wanted a washing that made him "whiter than snow."

That is the way it is with us. We all sin and we keep sinning. A bath once a year is like the yearly sacrifices in the Old Testament. It really doesn't cut it. Can we survive on a bath a year? I think so. Is that the abundant life for us, a life that attracts people to us? I don't think so.

That is why God has made it clear to us that we need to acknowledge that we sin, and when we sin, we need to confess it and be cleansed. We need to be like Gipper and accept the fact that spiritual baths are not only necessary, but they are good for us, for others, and for Him.

Some Gentle Reminders . . .

- Accept that you sin and will sin. Call sin for what it is. Make confession a way of life to both God and others. Clean bodies are refreshing. Be like Peter when Jesus was washing the feet of His disciples (**John 13:1–17**). Peter humbled himself and asked Jesus to wash not only his feet, but also his hands and head. Ask God to cleanse all of your life.

- God wants you to be clean more than you want it. He sent His Son, Jesus, who "got down and dirty" . . . experiencing the dirt of life. God knew we needed someone who could understand what we go through in this life. Jesus wants us to know that He understands and identifies with us. And the great thing is that He experienced the sins, but He did not sin. He shows us a better way.

- More importantly, He wants us to know that He took on all our sinful filth so that we could be forgiven. It is a once-and-for-all loving act. When He died on the cross, He took on all the sin of the world. He paid the price for our cleansing. When we accept that He paid the price for us, we are clean forever!

- And remember Who does all the work? God. It is God who provides the water, shampoo, and conditioner. And if the weather is cold, He will provide the hair dryer!
- And don't forget; you are like the rest of the human race. We all sin and get dirty. Confession is good for the soul. Find others who are humble about their own sins. Share, support, and encourage each other to take a bath!

Discussion Questions

1. What makes it tough for people to admit to a sin? What keeps us from admitting to others about sins in our lives?
2. Have you ever "paid a price" for confessing a sin? What did it cost you? Would you pay the price again?
3. Have you admitted to someone about a sin and were glad you told them? Why were you thankful that you confessed?
4. Why do you think God has a "system" of confession? How does it benefit you and others? Why is confession "good for the soul?"

5. Do you need courage to confess your sins in the presence of another person? Ask God for the courage to ask another person to be in your presence as you confess to Him.

12

Waiting on God

For from days of old they have not heard or perceived by ear, nor has the eye seen a God besides You, Who acts in behalf of the one who waits for Him (Isaiah 64:4).

In our garage is a study. That is where I spend time with my God. While I am with Him, outside the door I would often hear the clinking of dog tags, a plop, and then a groan that only a dog can give. There was Gipper with his head on the floor, waiting by a shut door. Waiting for me.

When I opened the door, we both were glad to see each other. There was tail wagging and talk reserved only for babies and dogs. If this was in the morning, it was a nice way to start the day—with your God and your dog.

As I repeatedly saw Gipper waiting by the study door, I realized that this is what God wants us to do—wait upon Him. There are many Bible verses that tell us, even command us, to wait upon God. It took a dog to remind me that this is what God wants for me as a way of life. I am to wait upon Him.

And what keeps me from waiting? Mostly fear or greed. The two factors that make the stock market go up and down are the two influences that cause me to not wait upon Him.

Whether it is waking up late, a list of things to do that is "too long," or anything else, there are many reasons that I don't wait. In fact, one reason I don't wait upon God is that I want to do His will my way. Like King David who was in a rush to get the ark to Jerusalem, I will be in a rush to do things my way . . . and it's all for Him! (**1 Chronicles 13:1–14**).

Has it gotten any easier over the years to wait upon God? Yes and no. Yes, I have learned the value of waiting. I have seen God's track record as I have waited. But there are times of testing. There is the test when the reward looks so good that I can't wait. Or there is the test when fear is so great I just can't take it any longer. Something has got to be done. The greater the reward, or the greater the price, the greater the test.

So what can we learn from a dog who waits outside the door of his owner?

Some Gentle Reminders . . .

- Waiting upon God is to be a way of life. We need to "fit" waiting into our schedule.

- Waiting is a command. We are commanded to wait upon God. He knows what is best for us and He knows how much time we have to get things done. Learn to trust Him for the "list" that does not end.
- The results of waiting on God are beyond our wildest expectations. In our finite ways of comprehending, we have no idea what God wants to do for those who wait for Him. He knows, and this is one of the reasons we are to wait.
- We wait on God, not on what He is to do for us. Gipper did not have a list of things for me to do. He was waiting on me, not on a bag of dog treats. We, too, are to do the same. We are to wait on God, not what we want Him to do.

Discussion Questions

1. What is the benchmark that people have for how much time is expected for God to come out of His "study?"
2. What does a person do as he/she waits upon God?
3. How does one get past the idea of waiting for what God can do for him/her and simply wait upon Him?
4. Just as we are to wait upon God, has He ever waited on you? What for?

5. What have been some of the rewards or blessings that you have experienced because you chose to wait on Him? How did God get the glory—looked good—because you waited?
6. Are you tired, frustrated, and just plain mad at waiting on God? What would you like for someone to do for you while the waiting continues?

13

Gipper and Fear

There is no fear in love; but perfect love casts out fear" (1 John 4:18).

The steadfast of mind You will keep in perfect peace, because he trusts in You (Isaiah 26:3).

It was an August day. The sky was dark and it was thundering. Carol was heading to the barn to treat her horse's hoof. As I was coming home, we met in the garage.

She said that Gipper was hiding under the steps, the steps that led from the garage to our den. He was afraid of the thunder. When I looked at Gipper, she was right. There was our dog underneath the steps, as close as he could get to a concrete wall, shivering in fear.

As Carol drove off, I called for Gipper. He would not move. I knew that it was safe for him to leave the garage because there was no rain or lightning, but he would not budge.

My mind looked for options. The first one was to crawl under the steps and drag him out. Common sense vetoed that one. Crawling under the steps is one thing.

Tugging on the collar of a 100+ pound dog was something else. I knew the collar would come with me. Not so sure about the dog.

Option two. I knew Gipper liked to be groomed. He could sit in our yard forever as we used two brushes (one for general brushing, the other for "detailed work") to comb his matted hair.

The routine for grooming was simple. I would take the two brushes, knock them together, and say to him, "Groom, groom." Whatever our dog was doing, he stopped and came to us. He knew what was in store for him. We then led him to the backyard and groomed him until our arms were tired. And how did the neighbors know Gipper had been groomed? There were golden wads of fur lying in our yard!

Knowing what Gipper loved, I found the two grooming brushes and knelt close to our fearful dog. Knocking them together, I said, "Groom, groom." I had his attention. With additional coaxing, Gipper got up and followed me to the backyard. Was it still thundering? Yes, but our quivering dog followed. He knew what was about to happen.

So there the two of us sat, with me on the steps of our deck and Gipper sitting close to me with his nose pointing upward, his signal that he was ready. And the grooming began.

As the thunder clapped, I kept grooming, calmly telling him that everything was all right. He did not need to be afraid. After several minutes of grooming, the shaking stopped and I had a dog that was no longer afraid.

All of us are like Gipper. There are times when we are afraid. Some fears are real. Others are perceived fears. For some of us, those fears do not go away. We are stuck with them, huddled under the steps of life. We pray and pray, "God, deliver me from all my fears" (**Psalm 34:4**) and nothing happens. And sometimes for me, I can't stop my fearful thoughts and feelings. God seems to be quiet.

When times like this happen, someone or something reminds me of a simple truth—there is no fear in love. God's perfect love casts out all my fears. (**1 John 4:18**). Like a child, I pray for God to intervene, to do something to let me know that He loves me.

That something is either an act of lovingkindness such as grooming brushes and a great groom, or it is a promise. He gently tells me to trust what He *will* do. I either see His hand act or His Spirit encouraging me to trust in His presence. I refocus. My attention moves from the thunder to keeping my eyes on Him who loves me.

For me, I need to know that God is with me and that He loves me. Sometimes that happens spontaneously. Other times, it is a sheer act of trust. Either way, when these two truths reach my heart, the fear subsides.

Some Gentle Reminders . . .

- An ongoing, day-to-day relationship with the Father keeps me aware that He loves me. Gipper and I had that kind of a relationship. Stay intentional with your time with Him. Position yourself to receive the good things (grooming) that He wants to do for you. Make time to be groomed. Stay close to God as a way of life.

- Address your fear. When the disciples saw Jesus walking on water during a storm, they were terrified because they thought He was a ghost. Peter spoke to Jesus and said, "If it is You, command me to come to you on the water." Jesus said, "Come" and Peter walked on water (**Matthew 14:26–29**). Peter trusted Jesus as to Who He was. His walking with Jesus on water was proof that Jesus was Jesus, not a ghost. Face your fears in the presence of God.

- And if you are like Peter, who begins to sink in the water because of the stormy circumstances in life, cry out to Jesus. Jesus stretched out His hand, lifted him out of the sea, and Peter continued to walk on water in a storm (**Matthew 14:30–33**). And what can the hand of God do when you are fearful? King David said, ". . . in Your hand is power and might; and it lies in Your hand to make great and to strengthen everyone" (**1 Chronicles 29:12**). Take hold of God when He reaches out to you.

- To break the cycle of fearful thoughts, I ask, "God, what do You have to say about this fear?" I then wait for whatever He reveals.

- We all need love. God knows this. That is why He loves us *first*. When we experience His love, we can love Him back (**1 John 4:19**). Loving and being loved in the presence of the God who controls everything is the antidote for fear. This love then allows faith and hope to remain in the midst of fear (**1 Corinthians 13:13**).

- The number one fear in life is the fear of being out of control. Ask God to show you how much He loves you and then reveal to you how much He is in control. If He shows you the "next righteous step," obey and continue to follow.

- When I am afraid, I sometimes make a list of what God has done to deliver me from my past fears. In the Psalms it is written: "Once again I'll go over what God has done, lay out on the table the ancient wonders; I'll ponder all the things you've accomplished, and give a long, loving look at your acts" (**Psalm 77:12**, The Message). This helps me have a "steadfast mind."

Discussion Questions

1. When was the last time you shared with someone about what makes you fearful? Can you tell at least one person about one fear that you have?
2. What are your thoughts about love as the antidote for your fears? Any exceptions or additional truths needed to overcome fear?
3. Leadership training tells leaders to stay calm around their followers during fearful situations. How do you stay calm when fear grips those around you?
4. What would you like others to do for you when you are fearful?
5. How does one get in touch with a loving God when fear runs amuck?

14

When Dogs Are "Bad Dogs"

For I know that nothing good dwells in me, that is, in my flesh; for the wishing is present in me, but the doing of the good is not. For the good that I wish, I do not do; but I practice the very evil that I do not wish (Romans 7:18–19).

It is not that parents think their child can do no wrong. More often, they think that the child cannot do a lot of wrong. It's to be expected that a child will misbehave in the classroom. It's the trip to the principal's office that catches them by surprise.

That's true of dog owners too . . . until something goes wrong big time with their dog's behavior.

For a parent, it happens somewhere between the "terrible twos" and adolescence. For the dog owner, it happens about seventy-two hours after their dog is part of the family.

It can be almost anything: the biggest hole that a dog could ever dig in the front yard, chewing on the furniture, or something that just causes you to yell the dog's first, middle, and last name!

Then something happens. Your dog is looking at you with no remorse or guilt. You are returning his/her stare with a glare and comments that are not repeatable on Facebook.

Three thoughts, something like this, runs through your mind:

- "Does my dog have any idea what this is going to cost me in time and money?"
- "Why would my pet do such a thoughtless, uncaring thing?"
- "Why does my dog not 'mind'? Why is there so much self-centeredness?"

Are there answers to these questions? Nope. Your dog has no idea what the costs will be. Your dog has no concept about selfishness. And the truth of the matter is that he/she does not pick up on your feelings for the recent behavior, unless you are sad or mad.

And that makes us, really mad!

At this point, a dog owner can respond in one of three ways.

- "This dog is going into a remedial dog obedience school first thing Monday morning!"
- "He just doesn't learn. How many more times will this happen? After all I have done, why does this continue to happen?"
- "I wonder if my aunt wants another dog?"

Frustration. Not knowing what to do next. The dog is one more problem on your growing list for the day. And at that moment, there is simply not a lot of love for the pet that could do almost no wrong.

So what can we learn from a misbehaving dog and an owner who is frustrated with his pet's behavior?

To be sure, and not carry the illustration of pet behavior too far, we need to keep in mind that we are not dogs and God is much more than a pet owner. But because all of us are born with the inclination to be alpha dog, to control our lives and have our way, there is an ongoing tension as to who will be in control—God or me.

Some Gentle Reminders . . .

- God understands everything there is to know about dogs and people. How many times have we tried to understand why our dog barks? There is never a "why" with God. He doesn't wonder why

dogs and people act a certain way. He understands everything about us.
- God doesn't run out of anything. He is never out of patience, money, time, and most of all, love. He is not limited, thus failing to give us what we need.
- God simply does not make mistakes. Unlike us, apologies are not needed because He failed on His part to do what was right. He is right every time when it comes to His dealings with us.
- God loves us more than a pet owner could ever love a pet. It is His perfect love that motivates Him to fill in the holes in the yard. It is His love that disciplines us for righteous behavior (**Revelation 3:19**). We do not have to fear that He will discipline in anger and "get carried away."

And the biggest difference between God and a dog owner? God has a much more effective way to change our lives and behavior.

Most dog owners know that behavior modification through rewards and punishments is the most effective way to change behavior. The major weakness of rewards and punishment is that it is an ongoing way of life. The pet must have "continuing education" for the desired behavior to remain. Withdraw these two influences and your pet reverts back to his old ways.

God tried to do the same and it did not work for a changed life. In the Old Testament, God made it very clear to His people about the way they were to live. In **Deuteronomy 28**, He said that He would reward them with blessings for godly behavior and punish them for misbehaving (sinning). All the blessings of the Promise Land and all the plagues of Israel's enemies did not make permanent changes.

The apostle Paul wrote, "For the good that I wish, I do not do; but I practice the very evil that I do not wish" (**Romans 7:19**). The Israelites knew that it was not within their efforts to be holy and stay holy. Efforts on their part, such as sacrifices, were needed continually.

God understood this. That is why He sent His Son to die for our sins. When we accept Christ into our lives, we receive a new spirit, the Holy Spirit. We are a new spiritual creation (**2 Corinthians 5:17**).

It is no longer up to us to respond to positive and negative reinforcements and hope a change takes place. God has literally put Himself within us. Because of a new being and the power of the Holy Spirit, we can *be* righteous and therefore *do* righteously. The struggle for controlling my life has an answer—Christ living in me.

This is something that Gipper never could experience. Apart from Christ, neither can you. And the new life is based upon a simple decision. Acknowledge that you have sinned. Acknowledge that only Christ can save you from yourself, your sin nature. And make the decision to accept Him as your savior.

Discussion Questions

1. What kind of pet behaviors drive you crazy? What has been your reaction? Did your reactions change your dog's behavior? What happened the next time that the very same thing happened?
2. What struggles (sinful misbehaving) continually plague you after using positive and negative rewarding? Any repeats? What thoughts and feelings are there when change does not take place?
3. What is your take on the idea that God wants to give you a new spiritual being? How have you allowed His life in you to change you so that a real difference will take place?

15
God's Care as We Age

I have been young and now I am old, yet have not seen the righteous forsaken or his descendants begging bread (Psalm 37:25).

Aging. It's something we see all around us. We talk about those who are aging around us. But if we talk about ourselves growing older, it is usually with some fear, anger, or regrets. We can slow it down, but no one can stop it.

During Gipper's later years, we paid more attention to the aging chart at his veterinarian's clinic. When he approached the "people age" of the 80s, we knew he was a senior dog!

The signs were clear: white around his nose, sleeping more, and the loss of hearing. When jogging with him, instead of his leading, we would be the one in the lead. Getting him into the backseat of the car was increasingly difficult. It took two of us to help, one whistling and encouraging, the other lifting his hind legs. What Gipper's veterinarian said when we first looked into getting Gipper came true: "Large breed dogs have problems with their hips as they age."

The nights were spent checking on him. Instead of his waking us up, we would go see about him. Why? Because at this point in his life, he had a way of wandering from his doghouse—the garage—into the yard. If we did not coax him back into the garage with bread, he would stay outside in the rain or cold.

We did what we could to help. We bought a more expensive dog food with joint supplements. Medication was prescribed for his arthritis. We were faithful to make sure that he took his "meds."

During his last two to three years of living, not once did I see Gipper worry. Not once did he beg for help with whimpering. There was such contentedness as his eyes met ours. I once said to him, "Gipper, I hope I can age as well as you."

So what does Gipper's aging have to do with yours and my aging? What did I learn about God as our dog increased in years?

Some Gentle Reminders . . .

- God does not forsake us as we age. As an old man, David, in **Psalm 37:25**, wrote that he had not seen the righteous or his descendants forsaken.

- As Carol and I cared for Gipper, I realized that God does the same for His own. He knows we all will die. He has made provisions for us. He will not forsake you.
- Be on the lookout for reminders about God's care for His creation. Jesus told us to look at the lilies of the field as a reminder to not worry (**Matthew 6:28**).
- God cares more for us than any dog owner will care for his pet. As we grow older, remember that God knows us well. He made us. He knows every cell in your body . . . the very number of hairs on your head (**Luke 12:7**). We are valuable to Him. He has all the resources needed for our care.
- God has a different "criteria" for successful productivity. Strength, energy, education, and intelligence are the world's requirements. But in God's kingdom, some of the most successful people did their best work as senior adults. Learn how God enabled them to be successful.

Discussion Questions

1. What stories do you have of pets being well cared for as they aged?
2. What kind of fears do you have of being cared for when you get older?

3. How do you respond to people who do not properly prepare for old age? How have you prepared yourself for when you will get older?
4. How does one prepare to trust God during the senior adult years?
5. What do you think were the "ingredients" for success for senior adults in the Bible? What happened in the lives of Abraham, Moses, Caleb, Elijah, and the apostle John that caused them to do their best work as they aged?
6. What role does righteousness (**Psalm 37:25**) have in God not forsaking us?

16

The Day Gipper Died

"O death, where is your victory? O death, where is your sting?" (1 Corinthians 15:55).

For the past several weeks, we knew that Gipper was in his last days. The "telling moment" was on Christmas Eve. We returned home from our church's candlelight service. The night was rainy. I called for Gipper, but there was no response.

With flashlight in hand, I walked through the backyard of our home, but no Gipper. Moving to the front yard, the light beam scanned the yard. There was Gipper, stuck in mud.

Located near the front door was one of the many holes that he took pleasure in digging. It was one of his favorite places during the summer heat, but on this rainy night it was a place where rain collected.

Gipper acknowledged us but did not move. Because of the deterioration of his hips due to arthritis, he could not get out of the mud. He needed help.

Within an hour's time, Carol and I went from a church sanctuary lit by hundreds of candles to standing in mud. We got two towels and put them under Gipper's body. Slowly we lifted him out of the mud and gently led him into the garage and then into my study. For some reason, I didn't care how much mud he tracked into the study. I was simply thankful to have found our dog. As I was cleaning the mud off his long coat of fur, I knew his days were numbered.

The next day was Christmas. Gipper had perked up and was moving around. As the family gathered in the dining room for our Christmas meal, Gipper was outside, looking into the dining room window. I ran for my camera and proceeded to take pictures of him, more than any other member of the family. I knew his time was short, and I wanted memories of his last Christmas with us.

So what was my best gift for Christmas? A dog that was alive.

Three weeks passed and Gipper grew steadily weaker. He went three days without eating. We would hold a bowl of water to his mouth so he could drink. Carol and I would use towels and a sheet to help him up. When he did walk, he would go outside the garage and simply lay in one spot. At nighttime, I would take a slice of bread—his favorite treat—and woo him back inside . . . or carry him.

On Wednesday night, January 14, Carol and I looked at each other and knew the "time was at hand." Gipper no longer recognized us. When we petted him, there was no wagging of his tail and no eye contact. For us to allow him to continue in this condition just so that we could have a pet would have been selfish.

Gipper's vet was contacted the next morning. We were ready to euthanize him. Because of his workload, Dr. Richard Hewitt left word for me to bring him to the clinic the next day, January 16.

On this morning, I slowly drove Gipper to the clinic. I did not want his feeble body to roll in the back of our van. When I arrived, I went inside to the waiting room. The receptionist knew the reason for my being there. Without a word, she gave me a form to sign. It authorized Richard to euthanize him. After signing it, I looked at the other adults seated. Each had a pet that was very much alive. All of them were there to help their pet get better. I was not. As I took a seat, I realized that I was the only one without a pet next to me. I dreaded the thought that one of them would ask me why I was there.

A brief meeting took place with Richard. He wanted to make sure that both Carol and I were in agreement to euthanize him. It was an eerie feeling as I gave a person permission to take the life of our dog.

Assistants and I then went to the van. We lifted Gipper onto a cart. I was told to wait in the van. They would call my cell phone. Not wanting to sit and wait, I went to the post office to mail a letter . . . something to do. As I returned to the clinic, Carol had pulled into the parking lot. I was most thankful to have her presence.

As we sat in the parking lot, my cell phone rang. It was Richard. He said he would bring the body to our home.

When he arrived, he and I lifted a green cloth bag out of the back of his truck and carried Gipper to his grave. I chose one of his favorite spots. [Remember that moment of eye contact that I spoke of earlier? This is where it took place.] During the hot summer months, Gipper liked to lie underneath a maple tree where it was cool. That was his final resting place.

One of the blessings was the fact that the grave was dug about three weeks earlier—the night before the temperature dipped to seven degrees. It would have been most difficult to dig a grave in frozen ground.

Richard was God's man for the hour. He reassured me that the grave was deep enough. I told him how awkward I felt sitting in the waiting room with other pet owners who were there for the health of their dogs, there to have their pet "fixed" in a good way, to be healthy. His response was God-given. He wisely told me that I *had* fixed him. "You have fixed him from having to suffer." Words of comfort. When Richard left, I felt that God had sent an angel in the form of a veterinarian.

The rest of the morning was spent covering Gipper's body with dirt. One of the memories that stays with me is of me blowing my nose from crying. I was most thankful for the solitude. The tears could flow with no shame of others seeing me. As I blew my nose, I tossed the Kleenex tissues into the grave. There was something symbolic about doing this, almost like a part of me was buried with him. Once the grave was filled, my last "act" was to take a GPS reading of the grave's location. I did not want a grave marker.

There was a peace. I walked into the house and pulled out Gipper's file. I recorded the GPS location, the date of his death, and his age—fourteen years and five months.

To gain closure on the fact that Gipper was no longer a part of our daily routine, I gathered his personal belongings. I emptied his water container. The old ragged throw rug that he slept on for years was tossed.

Everything that I knew to do was accomplished. I then took a blessed shower. I just stood there and soaked away the cold of the morning. By this time, it was 3:00 p.m. I hadn't eaten any breakfast or lunch. I was hungry, so I fixed one of my favorite sandwiches.

Carol came home at about 4:00 p.m. I was most thankful to have her in my life. We shared thoughts and feelings and then she went to feed her horse. I took a much-needed nap and then journaled, for a couple of hours, the events of the day. One of the entries was the blessings in Gipper's death—how God provided at every turn.

Here are some of the things He did:

1. For months leading to his death, I was fearful that Gipper, in his dementia, would wander from the house. He never did.
2. The week before Gipper's death, I pulled a muscle in my back. I had a lot of pain. How would I lift Gipper? God knew this and provided someone when Gipper's ninety-pound body needed to be lifted and lowered. Even as I tossed dirt on his grave, there was no pain.
3. And on the day Gipper was buried, the sun was shining!

Why did I give you the details of a dog's death and what his owner experienced? Simply put, all of us will have loses. Someday we all will lose those who we love. Or, we too will face death. Death has a way of taking away our ability to control. It can't be avoided. This is part of life.

What I experienced in the death of our dog is that God provides. He intervenes when we cannot control or fix things. And when He does this, we experience God.

The God who provides for a dog is the One who will provide for you.

Some Gentle Reminders . . .

- As we plan for losses in life, sometimes there are circumstances that we cannot control. This gives God the opportunity to intervene.
- God knows all your feelings and thoughts during times of loss. Stay honest with yourself and Him. Nothing catches Him unprepared. Watch what He does in the small things and the big ones.
- Stay connected with yourself and others. For myself, I needed a quiet weekend to be with my God and Carol.
- After some time has taken place, take time to record the blessings that you experienced with your pet. Someday a book may come out of it. Or at the right time and place, you may be led to share with someone how God has blessed you.
- Watch for ways to be comforted. God is the Father of mercies and *all* comfort. He wants to comfort us. Afterwards, be on the lookout to pass this same comfort on to others (**2 Corinthians 1:3–4**).

Discussion Questions

1. Have you lost a pet that you loved? If so, how did you prepare for the loss and what helped you get through this tough time?
2. If you had to euthanize a pet, what advice would you give to others about making that decision? How did you know when it was "the right time"?
3. Were there any special Bible verses or thoughts that God gave you that helped with the loss?
4. What blessings did you have from owning your pet? Would you do it "all over again" as a pet owner?
5. Was there any sting from the death of your pet? If so, can you share it with someone else?

17

What Are You Leaving Behind?

"A good person leaves an inheritance for their children's children . . ." (Proverbs 13:22, NIV).

Two Christmases have come and gone since the death of Gipper. For the second Christmas, Carol and I decided to give each other a new couch and chair. To make room, one of our two den recliners had to go. We decided that it would replace the recliner in my study.

Before our son and I moved the recliner from the den to the study, I dismantled the study recliner. It was going to a thrift store the next day. Removing the recliner back made it easier to transport it in the family van.

When the recliner back was removed, I was surprised by all the dog hair concealed in the crevices. How did it all get there?

Remember the story about Gipper moving from a three-foot-diameter doghouse to a two-car garage doghouse? Carol did not think that Gipper should have to face the elements of nature. He therefore quickly moved up the socio-economic ladder in the dog world, to our garage.

But this rapid ascent did not stop there. When the cold, wet weather was at its worst, Gipper got a new addition to his house—my study!

For you see, our daughter, Elisa, felt sorry for Gipper during the rainy winter season. She knew that my study not only had carpet, but it was connected to the house's central heating and cooling system. Before I could comprehend it, Gipper's doghouse had carpet and heat . . . just like our bedroom!

But it did not stop there . . .

Gipper was a smart dog. It did not take him long to learn that my recliner was more comfortable than the floor. When we would check in on him before bedtime, there he was on my recliner. He would either be in a regal pose, on his "throne," or he would be curled up in a golden fur ball with his head between his paws. Only a tug on his red collar would get him off my recliner.

The first few years I accepted the fact that my recliner was no longer my recliner. I would put up with a wet, stinky dog lying on it because it was a hand-me-down recliner. The black, vinyl covering was easy to clean.

The testing came when we inherited Carol's brother's nice, brown recliner, one that had cloth upholstery. Regardless of how many bed sheets we placed on it, Gipper, the dog with long, golden fur, made his presence known long after he left the study. It was the remnants of this fur that I found when disassembling the chair.

It seemed like hair was everywhere, in every crevice and underneath the frame. Knowing that someone else would be sitting where Gipper (and I) sat, I was not parting with the recliner until I took the shop vac to it.

As I was vacuuming, there was some frustration. *I am not having someone sit on my dog's hair. I want to clean up what Gipper left behind.* I know Gipper did not think once about my having to vacuum behind him. He was a dog and dogs shed their fur. But the reality is that most people do not want to sit on dog fur. It needs to be vacuumed. Someone has to clean up the dog fur of life. What he did was unintentional.

As I continued to vacuum, a second series of thoughts went through my mind. I began to recall the "good" fur stories, the feel-good memories. Whether we were jogging on a trail or Gipper was sitting in the back seat of the car as we stopped at the drive-through window of a restaurant, people would say, "What a beautiful dog you have." That made me proud.

There are some things that we will leave behind intentionally. My grandmother took many hours during her senior years to hand knit afghans for each of her four grandchildren. Though she died more than twenty years ago, we are still influenced by her efforts as we pull our afghans over us on cold nights.

Like her, you can deliberately leave something behind that is intentional. Or you may leave your "dog fur" that is unintentional. Either way, something will be left behind . . . and it will be good.

Sadly, we can also leave behind memories that are not good ones. The title of Clint Eastwood's movie, *The Good, the Bad, and the Ugly*, is a description of what we leave behind for others to remember. Because we are human, we can do damage that cannot be repaired. That is the ugly and bad.

It can be difficult to look at your life and discern what you will leave behind. However, God can give the wisdom that is needed to inventory your life. Ask Him for the grace to make needed changes. It will be a godly inheritance for another generation.

King Solomon wrote in Proverbs that a righteous person—a good will person—will leave an inheritance. What you leave behind could be for more than one generation. It could be for the children of your children. Your influence is not for the here-and-now. It is for those who live after you.

What reminders can we take from a dog that made himself at home on the recliner of his owner?

Some Gentle Reminders . . .

- We will leave behind an influence. Be it for good or bad, we will impact the lives of others.
- If you realize that someone will have to clean up "the fur" you left, remember the story of Joseph. Joseph's brothers deliberately sold their brother into slavery because of jealousy. Years later, God positioned Joseph to provide for them in Egypt during a time of famine. Joseph said to them, "As for you, you meant evil against me, but God meant it for good in order to bring about this present result, to preserve many people alive" (**Genesis 50:20**). What can be evil or bad, intentional or unintentional, can be used for the good of others. If you cannot undo what has been done, ask God to make something good out of it for others.
- The hair left by Gipper brought about pleasant memories because of what he was—a dog. Gipper did not try to be any other species of an animal. He was a dog. Be yourself as you influence others.
- Sometimes it does not take a lot to influence others. Gipper did not strive to shed his fur. It just happened. Little did he know that someday he would influence others in a story about his life.

Discussion Questions

1. If you are a pet lover, are there any good memories that your pet left behind? How did they influence your life?
2. Any regrets about what you might or will leave behind? Can you share one of them with another person? If not, can you be honest with God and ask Him to turn it into good?
3. What kind of God-legacy (inheritance) do you want to leave behind? Share this with others and ask for help.

Acknowledgments

The root meaning for "acknowledgment"[*] is a combination of an Old English word and a Middle English word—to know + recognize. I want to recognize those who I **know** played a God-given role in the writing of *The Gospel According to Gipper*.

With great appreciation, I recognize . . .

My God, who made all the resources and people available to me for me to write. It was Your truths and Your inspiration that began this journey. You have blessed me with a dog named Gipper. May You "look good" (be glorified) with the life of Gipper.

My wife, Carol. It was you who first read each chapter and offered suggestions. Little did I know that I needed someone like you to help care for our dog. Blessings on you!

Our children, Elisa and Chris. To you, Elisa, for helping "dear old Dad" know what computer keys to push to get the manuscript to the publisher. If Gipper were around, he would appreciate your advocating my study as an addition to his doghouse! To you, Chris, for giving me a letter with "gentle reminders" as I traveled on a

---

[*] The source for the root meaning is www.dictionary.reference.com

mission trip to South Africa. Your gentle reminders influenced me to pass "gentle reminders" on to the readers.

Kent Crockett. You were the one who God used to introduce me to the world of writing. I thank God for your walking alongside of me, chapter by chapter, as I wrote.

Terry Bailey, Darya Crockett, and Yvonne Parks, staff of Innovo Publishing. Terry, I will always be thankful for your husband, Greg, for telling me of your work at Innovo. It was you who sold me on the godly niche that Innovo has in the world of Christian publishing. Darya, God has gifted you with "getting in the head of a writer" to help him communicate from the heart. Your encouragement in editing my rough drafts has earned you a special place in heaven! Yvonne, your cover design wows a writer. You know how to make a dog look good! Blessings on each of you and your work with other Christian writers.

Sandra Valentine, the co-worker who told me about Gipper. You were the one who knew the Haddens were giving away their dog. The first time you asked me about owning a dog I said, "I don't have time for one." I am most thankful that you made a second attempt to tell me about Gipper. There were thirteen years of "golden" blessings because you asked a second time if I wanted a dog!

Richard Hewitt, Gipper's veterinarian. You were the one who took care of Gipper's "ailments" for thirteen years. I appreciate, more than you know, your being in his life for thirteen years, especially the day he died.

John and Linda Hadden, the former owners of Gipper. You may be at the end of the acknowledgments, but you were at the beginning of my life with Gipper. You wanted to give Gipper away for free so that you could pick out the next owners for him. I greatly appreciate your selection of owners!

CPSIA information can be obtained at www.ICGtesting.com
Printed in the USA
LVOW100722261111

256536LV00001B/3/P